The Monster of Moon 5

Paul Shipton

Illustrated by

David Mostyn

OXFORD
UNIVERSITY PRESS

In the Rocket-Bus

Some of the children were going camping on Moon 6.

"It says in my book that Moon 6 is very nice," said Vish.

Mr Potts aimed the rocket-bus
at the moon.
“Slow down!” shouted Miss Ock.
“We’re going to...”

With a crunch, the rocket-bus landed on top of a hill.

The teachers had a look at the bus.
"I think it's broken," said Mr Potts.
"But I can fix it."
"No!" said Miss Ock. "*I'll* fix it."

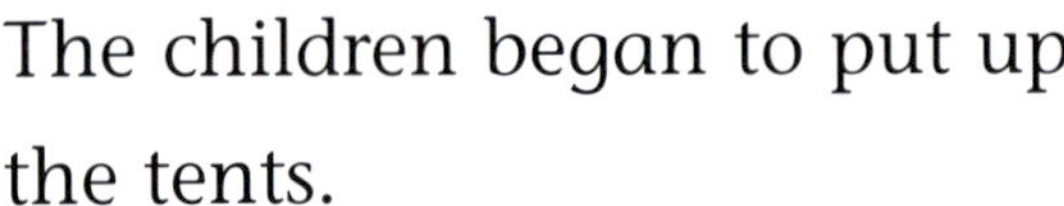

The children began to put up the tents.
"It's very dark here," said Vish.
"My book says that Moon 6 is bright."

It must be night.

"Let's make a fire," said Mr Potts. He asked Nick and Blop to go and get some sticks. They set off for the trees at the bottom of the hill.

Vish went on looking at her book. "Oh no!" she cried. "We've made a mistake!"

She ran to Miss Ock, who was still trying to fix the bus.
"This isn't Moon 6," cried Vish.
"We're on Moon 5!"

"What does the book say about Moon 5?" asked Miss Ock.

"Nobody has been here for a long, long time," Vish read out. "Some people say there are monsters here!"

The teachers got all the children together.

"We have to leave now!" said Mr Potts.

"We can't leave until I fix the bus," said Miss Ock. She gave Mr Potts a cross look.

"What about Nick and Blop?" asked Vish. "They're not back yet."

"I'll have to go and get them," said Mr Potts. "You wait in the tent."

The teacher ran off down the hill.

IN THE FOREST

Nick and Blop were deep in the forest looking for sticks. Suddenly, they heard a noise.

"Something's coming!" said Blop.
It was true! There was something in the trees. The two friends hid.
Don't say anything.

But it was just Mr Potts.

"Come quickly, boys!" he cried.

"We have to leave this moon!"

The three began to run back.

On the way, Blop tripped and fell in the mud.

“Ow! My foot hurts!” he said. Nick and Mr Potts had to pick him up and carry him.

IN THE TENT

The rest of the children were very afraid. Slig was telling them about the Monster of Moon 5.
"It's very big," he said, "and it's got long, sharp teeth."

Suddenly, they heard a noise outside the tent. "Something's coming!" said Vish.

The children ran out of the tent.

Something was coming up the hill. "It's the monster of Moon 5!" Lug cried. "Run!"

"Wait!" shouted Nick, but there were too many screams and nobody heard him.

Miss Ock had just finished fixing the bus.
"At last!" she said. "Now we can go!"

But then Lug ran right into the light. It fell and smashed.

Now it was so dark that nobody could see at all.

Miss Ock turned on a second light. "There's nothing to be afraid of," she said. "It's just Mr Potts and the boys."

"Wait!" said Vish. "We're on a hill, but it says in my book that there *are* no hills on Moon 5!"

Suddenly, the hill moved.
"This *isn't* a hill! We're on the monster!" cried Vish.
They all ran to the bus.

Two big eyes opened. It was the monster, and it was looking at them.

The monster roared and snapped, but the bus was too fast for it. Miss Ock was driving now!